CW00340518

BRAIN DETECTIVE

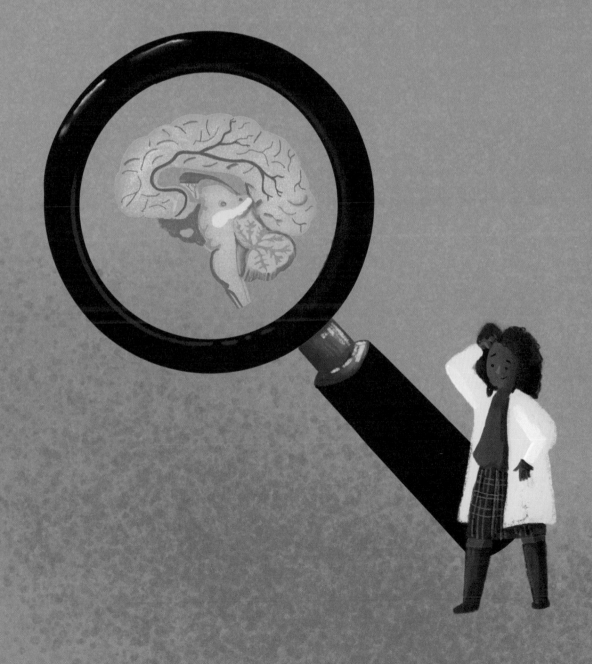

For my dad, who encouraged
me to ask questions.
T.J.

To Fionn, for those questions I didn't have
the answer to, I hope this helps.
A.C.

First published in Great Britain in 2023 by Wren & Rook

Text copyright © Tim James, 2023
Illustration copyright © Aaron Cushley, 2023
Design copyright © Hodder & Stoughton Limited, 2023
All rights reserved.

The right of Tim James and Aaron Cushley to be identified as the author and illustrator respectively of this
Work has been asserted by them in accordance with the Copyright, Designs & Patents Act 1988.

ISBN: 978 1 5263 6394 7
E-book ISBN: 978 1 5263 6395 4
10 8 6 4 2 1 3 5 7 9

C - 3PO ® is a registered trademark of Lucasfilm Entertainment Company Ltd.
Disneyland ® is a registered trademark of Disney Enterprises, Inc. KitKat ® is a registered
trademark of Nestlé Hershey. Monopoly ® is a registered trademark of Hasbro, Inc.
Pikachu ® is a registered trademark of Nitendo of America Inc.

MIX
Paper from
responsible sources
FSC
www.fsc.org
FSC® C104740

Wren & Rook
An imprint of Hachette Children's Group
Part of Hodder & Stoughton
Carmelite House, 50 Victoria Embankment, London EC4Y 0DZ

An Hachette UK Company
www.hachette.co.uk
www.hachettechildrens.co.uk

Printed in China

No part of this publication may be reproduced, stored in a retrieval system, or transmitted, in any form or by
any means, without the prior permission in writing of the publisher, nor be otherwise circulated in any form
of binding or cover other than that in which it is published and without a similar condition including this
condition being imposed on the subsequent purchaser.

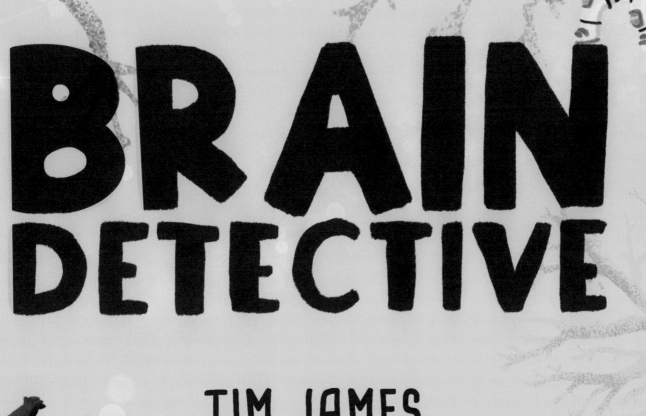

BRAIN
DETECTIVE

TIM JAMES

ILLUSTRATED BY
AARON CUSHLEY

wren
&rook

THE BIGGEST MYSTERY IN THE ROOM

Right now, you're using the most complicated computer in the world! It contains about 100 billion wires with more than 100 trillion links between them – that's more connections than the entire internet has. If you laid all those wires out end to end they would stretch for 176,000 km, which is long enough to wrap around the world four times. Yet the whole thing runs on 20 watts of power, one third of what you need for a light bulb. While we have learnt a lot about the brain, there are still so many things we don't know. In fact, the human brain is one of science's biggest mysteries.

It's the part of your body that tells everything else what to do, and it's the place where information about the world gets received and understood. Your body is just a vehicle – your brain is who you really are.

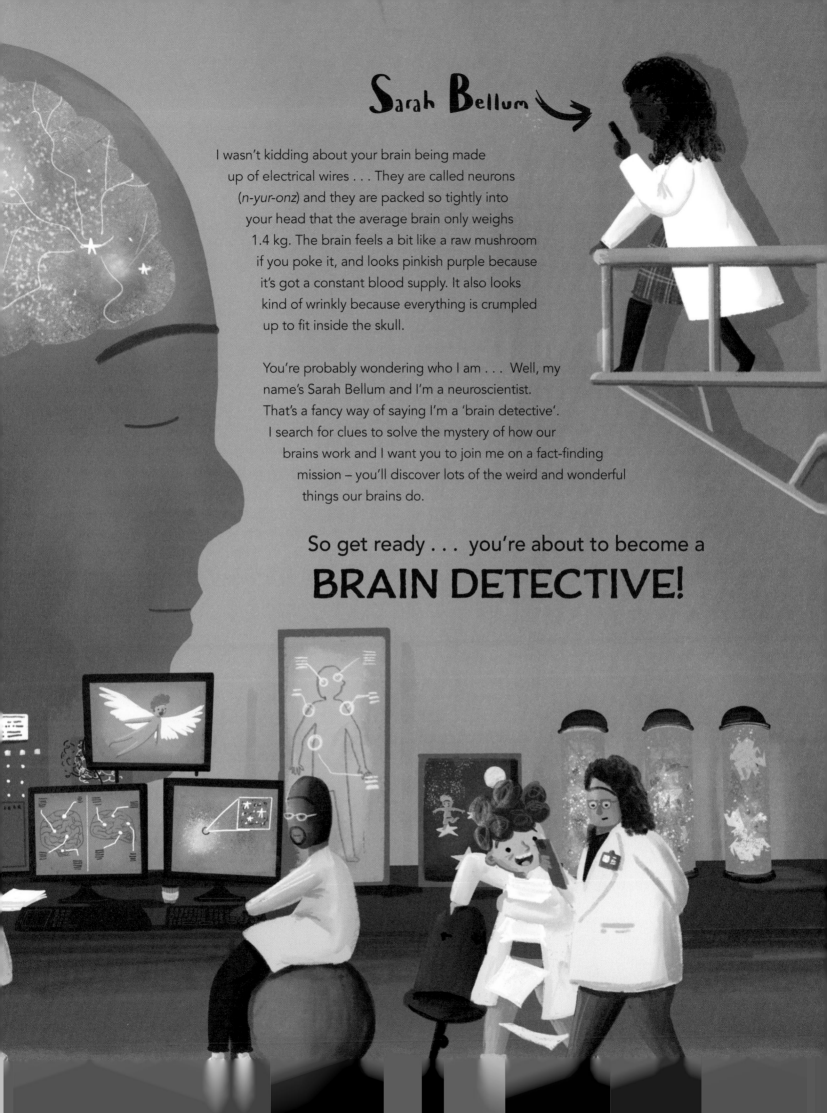

Sarah Bellum

I wasn't kidding about your brain being made up of electrical wires . . . They are called neurons (*n-yur-onz*) and they are packed so tightly into your head that the average brain only weighs 1.4 kg. The brain feels a bit like a raw mushroom if you poke it, and looks pinkish purple because it's got a constant blood supply. It also looks kind of wrinkly because everything is crumpled up to fit inside the skull.

You're probably wondering who I am . . . Well, my name's Sarah Bellum and I'm a neuroscientist. That's a fancy way of saying I'm a 'brain detective'. I search for clues to solve the mystery of how our brains work and I want you to join me on a fact-finding mission – you'll discover lots of the weird and wonderful things our brains do.

So get ready . . . you're about to become a
BRAIN DETECTIVE!

ANCIENT INVESTIGATORS

In every investigation, the first thing you've got to do is see what clues have already been uncovered. Fortunately for us, brain detectives have been at it for a few thousand years, although some of their experiments were a bit gross! Hope you've got a strong stomach . . .

Ouch!

MINDS OF MUMMIES

The first people to get a glimpse of a human brain were the ancient Egyptians. A papyrus (a material a bit like paper) written 3,700 years ago describes a man who got into an accident and wound up with a hole in his head, allowing people to stare inside and see the gooey mess.

The ancient Egyptians named what they saw 'the skull guts' because it looked similar to intestines, but they didn't have a clue what it did. They just knew it was slimy, so they figured its job was to make mucus and saliva that dripped down into the nose and mouth. Nice.

In fact, they were so unimpressed with the brain that when a person got mummified, their brain was yanked out with a hook through a hole made above the nose. This means that in ancient Egyptian stories, everyone in the afterlife walked around with their brain missing.

GETTING HOT IN HERE?

A thousand years after the Egyptians, the ancient Greeks decided the brain was a radiator that controls body temperature. They believed that a person's thoughts were stored inside the heart or liver – the reasoning for this was that the heart is in the middle of the body and the liver is really big, so they thought they were both more important.

MEDIEVAL MYSTERIES

In the Middle Ages, brain detectives began to figure out that the brain controlled who you were. They noticed that people who suffered head injuries started acting differently.

A tenth-century doctor named Al-Zahrawi performed surgery on men who had too much fluid in the brain, which made them act sleepy. He invented a drill that could pierce through the skull to drain the fluid. He then sewed up the wounds with bits of goat intestine. Gross! This probably goes without saying, but don't try this at home!

A HOLE IN THE HEAD

The curious case of Phineas Gage gave brain detectives a big clue about how the brain controls personality. In 1848, Phineas was laying dynamite to clear ground for a train-track when it accidentally exploded. The blast shot an iron pole right through the bottom of his head, and it came flying out the top, along with his right eyeball and a tiny chunk of brain. It doesn't sound like it, but Phineas was actually lucky because the metal was so hot it burned the wound on his head shut, stopping him from losing blood and ensuring his survival.

Phineas recovered, but his personality became completely different. Previously, he had been a hard-working, focused, cheerful fellow, but afterwards he became short-tempered, lazy and foul-mouthed. I'm not surprised – I doubt I'd be Miss Jolly Pants if someone exploded a metal pole through my face!

THE HIDDEN CITY IN YOUR HEAD

Every detective knows it's important to be familiar with the layout of the mystery they're trying to solve. We're trying to solve the mystery of the brain, so we should probably get our bearings a bit. We're going to need a map for this!

BRAIN DISTRICTS

If you ball up both your hands into fists and press them together, that's roughly how big your brain is. Inside your brain, billions of brain cells called neurons send electrical signals that zip around like cars in a busy city.

The brain is divided into chunks, each in charge of different things. This map shows what your brain would look like if we chopped right down the middle of your head. (Probably best that you don't actually do this to anyone.)

CEREBRUM

This big wrinkly bit on top takes up 80 per cent of the overall brain and is called the cerebrum (suh-ree-brum). This is where all your important thinking goes on.

BRAINSTEM

The brainstem sits at the bottom like the stalk of a flower, and it actually runs all the way down your back inside your spine. It's in charge of the simple stuff you don't have to deliberately think about, such as breathing, blinking, coughing, vomiting, reflexes, sneezing and sleeping.

CEREBELLUM

This bit here is called the cerebellum (pronounced Sarah Bellum, so obviously my favourite part). It sits just above your neck and it's in charge of your balance and movement. That's why getting hit on the back of the head makes you feel dizzy and fall over – you've just whacked the part in charge of controlling movement.

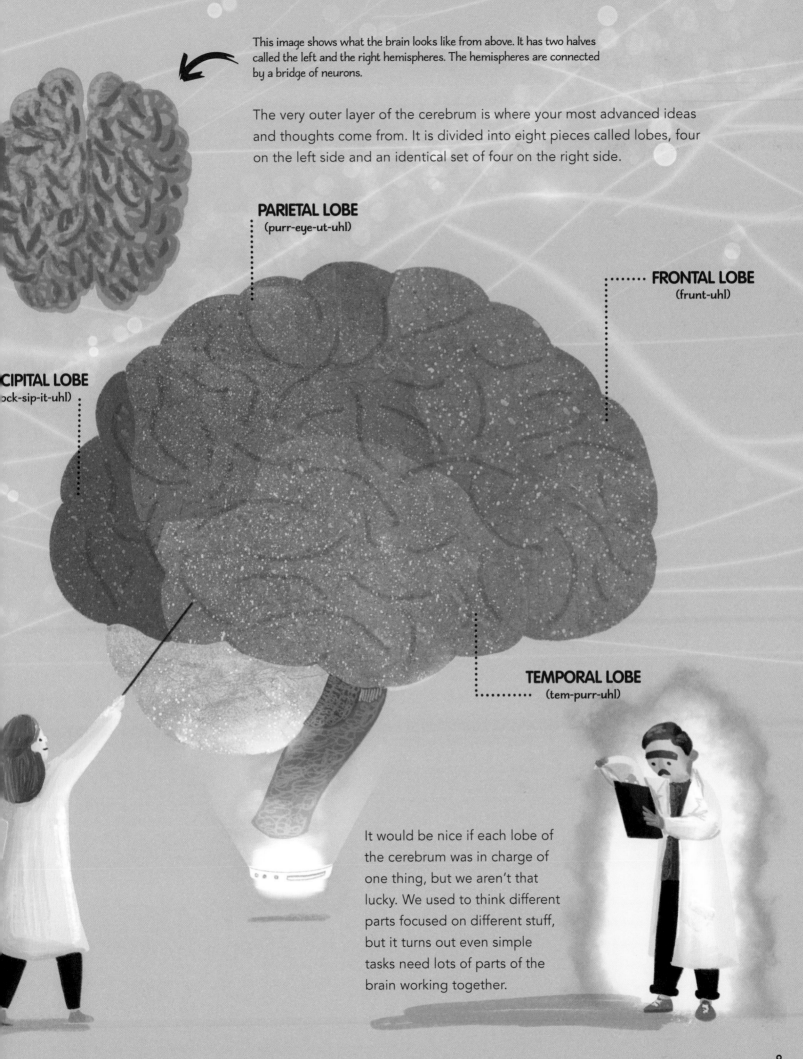

This image shows what the brain looks like from above. It has two halves called the left and the right hemispheres. The hemispheres are connected by a bridge of neurons.

The very outer layer of the cerebrum is where your most advanced ideas and thoughts come from. It is divided into eight pieces called lobes, four on the left side and an identical set of four on the right side.

PARIETAL LOBE
(purr-eye-ut-uhl)

FRONTAL LOBE
(frunt-uhl)

CIPITAL LOBE
(ock-sip-it-uhl)

TEMPORAL LOBE
(tem-purr-uhl)

It would be nice if each lobe of the cerebrum was in charge of one thing, but we aren't that lucky. We used to think different parts focused on different stuff, but it turns out even simple tasks need lots of parts of the brain working together.

THE BRAIN UNDER A MAGNIFYING GLASS

It's about time we took a sneak peek at neurons close up because they run the show. We're going to have to really zoom in for this because each one is only 0.1 millimetres wide – that's so small you could line 120 of them up side by side and they'd fit on just one fingernail! They look something like this . . .

WHAT'S GOING ON?

This weird tadpole-looking thing is a neuron. The blobby bit at the end is called the soma and is where chemical reactions take place.

Impulses carried toward cell body.

AXON
The electric shock gets blasted down this thread-like part of the neuron, called the axon, at 120 metres per second (four times faster than a car speeding on a motorway).

DENDRITES
The signal arrives at branches called dendrites. Most neurons have more than 10,000 dendrites, but most are too small to see, even with a magnifying glass!

NUCLEUS
The nucleus is in charge of building the cell and telling the other parts what to do.

SOMA
Neurons are surrounded by salty water. When tiny holes in the soma open and close, some water gets sucked inside, creating a tiny electric shock.

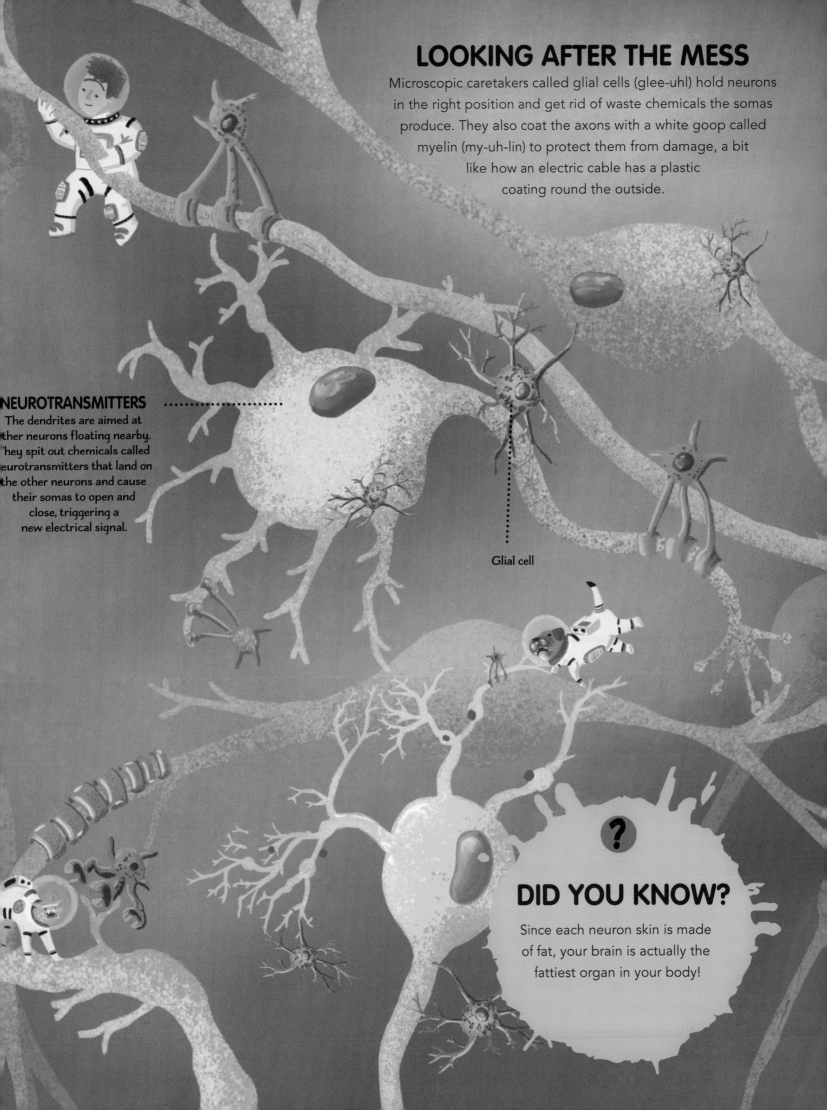

LOOKING AFTER THE MESS

Microscopic caretakers called glial cells (glee-uhl) hold neurons in the right position and get rid of waste chemicals the somas produce. They also coat the axons with a white goop called myelin (my-uh-lin) to protect them from damage, a bit like how an electric cable has a plastic coating round the outside.

NEUROTRANSMITTERS

The dendrites are aimed at other neurons floating nearby. They spit out chemicals called neurotransmitters that land on the other neurons and cause their somas to open and close, triggering a new electrical signal.

Glial cell

? DID YOU KNOW?

Since each neuron skin is made of fat, your brain is actually the fattiest organ in your body!

CLUES FROM BEYOND THE GRAVE

Investigating the brain can be tricky. People are usually busy using them, and don't like it when you crack their skull open to take a peek. This means some of the best clues about the brain come from dead bodies, which don't put up as much of a fight!

Let me see inside your brain!

DOCTOR OF DEATH

Back in the 1500s, it was illegal to cut open dead people and study their insides (the 1500s were no fun). Andreas Vesalius, one of the earliest brain detectives, decided to be a bit naughty. He wanted to know exactly what was going on inside the body – so in 1543, he began secretly digging up corpses and sneaking them back to his lab.

Vesalius became good friends with King Philip II of Spain, who agreed to change the law and give doctors and scientists permission to perform autopsies – that's where you cut open a dead body to try and figure out what's going on inside it.

Vesalius discovered that all the nerves in the body wind up connecting to the brain. When you touch or see something, your skin and eyes send electrical signals up those nerves to the brain where they get decoded and you figure out what's going on.

I'm looking for some body!

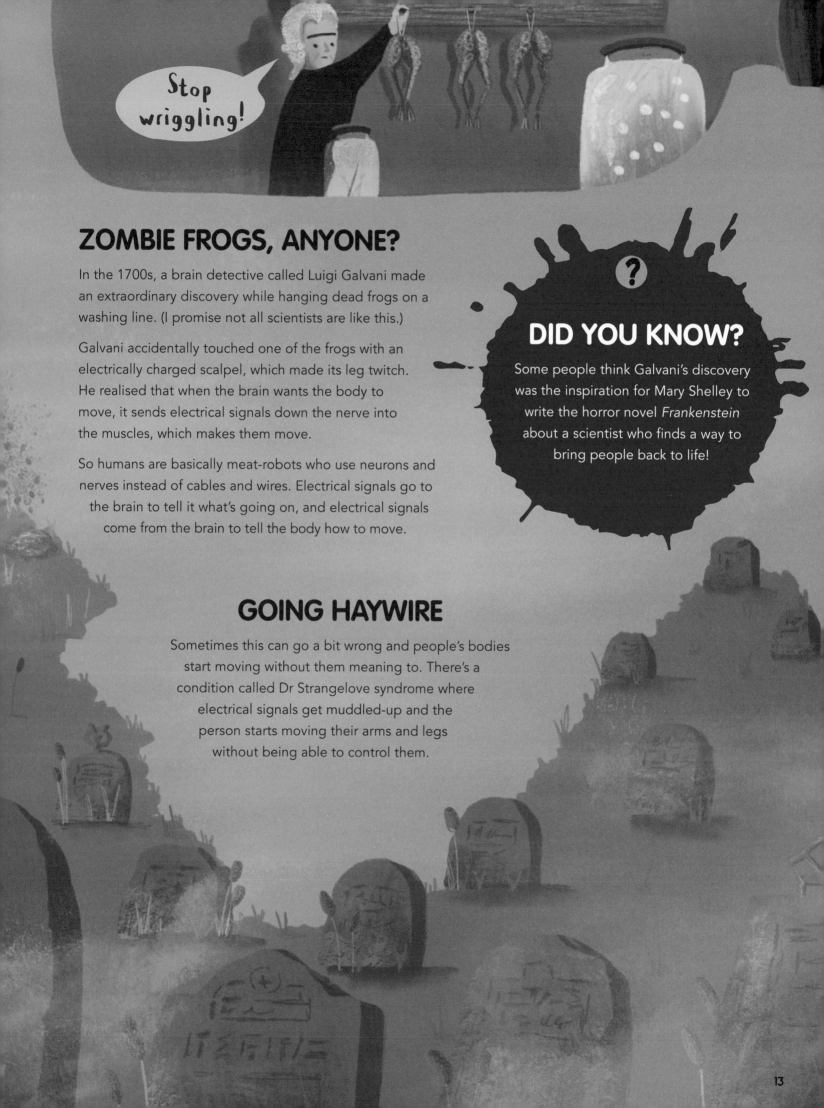

ZOMBIE FROGS, ANYONE?

In the 1700s, a brain detective called Luigi Galvani made an extraordinary discovery while hanging dead frogs on a washing line. (I promise not all scientists are like this.)

Galvani accidentally touched one of the frogs with an electrically charged scalpel, which made its leg twitch. He realised that when the brain wants the body to move, it sends electrical signals down the nerve into the muscles, which makes them move.

So humans are basically meat-robots who use neurons and nerves instead of cables and wires. Electrical signals go to the brain to tell it what's going on, and electrical signals come from the brain to tell the body how to move.

DID YOU KNOW?

Some people think Galvani's discovery was the inspiration for Mary Shelley to write the horror novel *Frankenstein* about a scientist who finds a way to bring people back to life!

GOING HAYWIRE

Sometimes this can go a bit wrong and people's bodies start moving without them meaning to. There's a condition called Dr Strangelove syndrome where electrical signals get muddled-up and the person starts moving their arms and legs without being able to control them.

CAMERAS IN YOUR FACE

The brain is in charge of taking in information about the world and piecing it all together into something we can understand, a bit like solving a case. Vision is one of the best examples of this – trillions of light particles enter your eyeball every second, but you're still able to make sense of it all and figure out what you're looking at!

I like to imagine the eye is a bit like a webcam. The wire that goes from the camera into the computer is like the optic nerve and the visual cortex is the computer itself.

A layer of tissue at the back of an eyeball called the retina is covered in tiny cells that are sensitive to light. When these cells get activated by light, they send electrical signals along the optic nerve to a place at the back of the brain in the occipital lobe called the visual cortex.

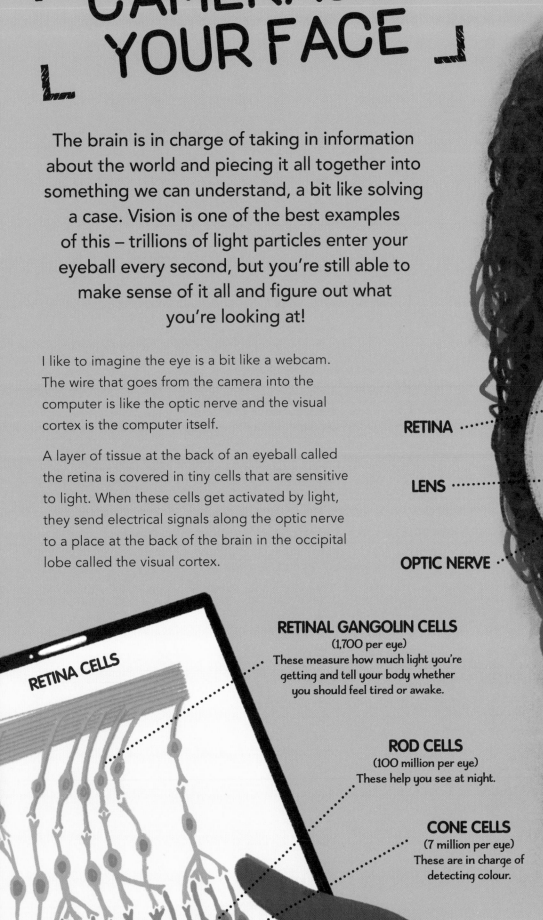

RETINA

LENS

OPTIC NERVE

RETINA CELLS

RETINAL GANGOLIN CELLS
(1,700 per eye)
These measure how much light you're getting and tell your body whether you should feel tired or awake.

ROD CELLS
(100 million per eye)
These help you see at night.

CONE CELLS
(7 million per eye)
These are in charge of detecting colour.

VISUAL CORTEX
The visual cortex is made of 140 million neurons and it's where your brain decides what you're looking at. It can understand 12 images per second.

CASE STUDY

Broken Mirrors of the Mind

In 1943, a Russian soldier named Lev Zasetsky was shot in the back of the head during a battle. The wound was very small. However, after waking up in hospital, Lev discovered he could no longer see the right side of any objects, including his own body or other people's faces. Whenever he looked at something, the right half of it was fragmented like a shattered mirror. The weird thing is that his eyes had been unharmed by the bullet, so even though they were doing their jobs, the part of his brain in charge of putting the information together simply wasn't.

? DID YOU KNOW?

If you play images faster than twelve per second, your brain can't keep up and thinks the images are moving. Early cartoon makers realised this and decided to make animated films play at twelve drawings per second, with each drawing shown twice to make it look less flickery – this is called 24 frames per second. This tricks the brain into seeing movement!

THE BRAIN ON STANDBY

Over the course of your life, you'll spend about 26 years asleep! (Not all at the same time of course.) It might surprise you, but sleeping is one of the main things our brain does. Even brain detectives need a rest from time to time. So what's going on when we're taking a snooze?

WHY DO WE SLEEP?

Nobody is sure exactly why we sleep. The most likely explanation is that it's a chance for our brains to clean themselves. During the day our neurons go through chemical reactions, which results in a build-up of toxic by-products. Eventually, these chemicals get too much and we need to shut everything down for a few hours to give our glial cells a chance to rinse everything out. Jellyfish, bullfrogs and young dolphins don't need sleep, but every human being does.

WHAT IS YOUR BRAIN UP TO AT NIGHT?

There are two main types of sleep, and your brain switches between them four or five times a night. Deep sleep is when your brain is clearing out the toxins. Rapid eye movement (REM) sleep is when you start to dream and your eyes dart around quickly under your eyelids. You can tell from watching a sleeping person's face which type they're experiencing by seeing if their eyes are jittering or not. I mean, obviously you should ask permission first. Don't just sneak into someone's bedroom and sit staring at them . . . I learned that one the hard way.

Everyone with a healthy brain dreams most nights, including people who are blind or visually impaired, who often experience dreams made of sound.

?

DID YOU KNOW?

The record for staying awake is held by a woman named Maureen Weston, who lasted 18 days and 17 hours without sleeping. At the same time, she set the record for the longest time spent in a rocking chair.

I can stay awake for ages!

WHY DO WE DREAM?

Nobody knows why dreams happen, but we know that every part of the brain is active during a dream, but the frontal lobes are the least active. The frontal lobes are the parts in charge of making decisions about what's going on, which is why you don't normally realise you're dreaming. The part of your brain in charge of going 'hmmm that's strange' is not fully alert.

This is a very weird dream!

I didn't mean it!

CASE STUDY

The Case of the Innocent Murderer

This case really is as spooky as it sounds! In 1987, a Canadian man named Kenneth Parks went to court because he killed his step-mother. What made this an unusual case is that Parks had committed the murder in his sleep! About one in three people sleepwalk, but Parks was the first person known to have sleep-murdered. In the end, the jury decided that since Parks hadn't been awake when the crime was committed, he was not guilty. You might have heard it's not safe to wake a sleepwalker, but this isn't true at all and actually it's a good idea to wake someone sleepwalking before they accidentally hurt themselves. Plus, their step-mother might thank you.

WHAT YOUR NOSE KNOWS

It's no surprise your brain needs a rest sometimes – it's so busy! One of the senses it's in charge of decoding (even when you are asleep) is your sense of smell. How exactly does the brain decide what something smells like? It's time to sniff out some clues!

OLFACTORY RECEPTORS
Smell-detector cells.

Waft!

WHY DO THINGS SMELL?

An object giving off a smell releases tiny bits of chemicals (called molecules) into the air that get sucked up our noses when we breathe. When these chemicals reach our nostrils they get dissolved into mucus, where smell-detector cells identify them.

These detector cells then send electrical signals to the brain. There are 10 to 20 million neurons in charge of deciding what you're smelling and what it means. You can actually detect at least one trillion different scents and smell is also the sense your memory hangs onto for the longest.

OLFACTORY NERVE
Takes information to the brain.

The Deadly Smell

In 1889, a factory in Frieburg, Germany, making the chemical propane-2-thione had a leak and the gas leaked out. The result was chaos. People who smelled it in the nearby town began vomiting, choking and falling unconscious. The smell was a bit like rotting eggs or the average PE changing room, only a hundred times worse.

Eughh!

Sniff

FAMOUS SMELLS

GEOSMIN
The smell you get after it's been raining (caused by bacteria in the soil).

Splash!

1-OCTEN-2-ONE,
The smell you get on your fingers after handling coins (caused by metal reacting with oil on your skin).

YUM!
The smell of baking bread (caused by more than 20 different chemicals).

? DID YOU KNOW?

In case you're wondering, the smell of a swimming pool is not caused by the chlorine people add to kill bacteria. It's caused by chlorine reacting with human sweat and urine. So, if you're in a swimming pool and you detect that horrible stinging fragrance, it means someone (or maybe a bunch of people) have been pool-peeing. Just felt that was an important fact to share.

Mmm

DRUM IN THE SKULL

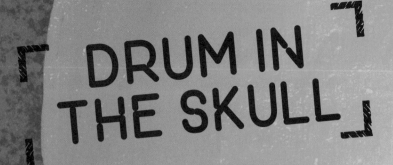

Ears are pretty amazing aren't they? Those shell-shaped things sticking out the sides of your head each contain about 15,000 tiny hairs that wobble when they detect a sound. They then send electrical signals into your auditory (or-dit-ree) cortex, which then get translated into sound information.

Bang! Bang!

HOW DOES SOUND WORK?

Banging a drum makes the tight skin surface vibrate (move very fast to and fro) and this makes the air particles around it vibrate. Those air particles bump into other nearby particles, and so on, until air particles in your ear start to vibrate too.

AUDITORY CORTEX
Located in the temporal lobes, the auditory cortex processes the signals as sounds.

**AUDITC
NERVE**
Nerves ca
signals to
brain.

EAR DRUM
Tympanic membrane (tim-panic) vibrates when airwaves hit.

COCHLEA
This tiny organ tu
the vibrations in
electrical signal

LET'S LOOK INSIDE

Just inside your ear is a thin layer of skin that vibrates like a drum when airwaves hit it. This drum is attached to another tiny organ inside your head that turns the drum vibrations into electrical signals. The signals travel along nerves into the brain. This is how we get sound.

The Sound that Caused a Toilet Queue

In 1993, when the sci-fi movie *Alien 3* was shown to a test audience, the film-makers noticed some people were getting up and leaving during the opening credits. But it wasn't because they didn't like the film. One of the notes on the movie's soundtrack was so low it was causing people's bowels to vibrate, which made them want to go to the toilet! And no, I'm not going to tell you how to recreate this note at home.

WHAT NOISE?

As you get older, you'll notice fewer high-pitched sounds. There are even special anti-children sirens, which make high-pitched whines that irritate kids and teenagers but don't affect old people because they simply can't hear them. Charming.

I'm desperate!

Me too!

Eeeeek!

HIGH AND LOW

Some sounds' vibrations are too low or too high for the human ear to detect. The average person can't hear lower than 20 vibrations per second or above 20,000 per second, but some animals can. This is why dogs can hear dog whistles, but humans can't.

?

DID YOU KNOW?

Usually ear damage causes deafness, but weird stuff can happen to the auditory cortex in the brain, leading to unusual types of hearing. The biologist Charles Darwin and former US president Theodore Roosevelt both had a condition called 'amusia'. They could hear every note in a piece of music, but were unable to detect a tune and just heard it as noise.

THE BRAIN'S HARD DRIVE

Your brain does a lot more than just detect things about the world around you. It can also store facts, memories and feelings for decades! It's like the ultimate evidence locker. Although storing memories is one of the most mysterious things the brain does, we have a few clues about how it does it . . .

HIPPOCAMPUS
The brain stores memories in the hippocampus.

I know it all!

CASE STUDY

Stuck in the Past

The hippocampus is in charge of organising all the information that makes up a memory. We know this from the case of Henry Molaison. He had a surgery in 1953 that accidentally removed part of his hippocampus and froze his mind in that year. Henry had a normal memory of everything up until his surgery, but he couldn't form new memories afterward. He lived in a constant timewarp, believing himself to be a 27-year-old man in the year 1953, even when he was an 82-year-old man in the year 2008.

The Man Who Knew Everything

Having part of your brain missing isn't always a bad thing. In fact, in some rare cases it can even help your memory, as with the mysterious Kim Peek. Although Kim was incapable of tying his own shoelaces or dressing himself, Kim had a perfect memory. He could read eight books a day and remember every fact in them, he could tell you what day of the week any date in history was, and could give you the postcode of any street in the world. Kim's memory was amazing but bizarrely, his brain was missing the corpus callosum, the bridge that connects the hemispheres.

DID YOU KNOW?

Nobody has any idea how memories are made or stored yet. We know that the electrical information is stored all over the brain, and we know the brain can store about 2.5 petabytes of data. If your brain was a computer hard drive, it could store about 100 years' worth of MP4s!

CASE STUDY

The Man Who Knew Too Much

Russian taxi driver Solomon Shereshevsky was capable of memorising 70-digit number grids, replaying conversations people had around him word for word, and copying out complicated science equations he had looked at once 16 years previously. Unfortunately for him, his memory also gave him face blindness (known as prosopagnosia). Whenever he met someone, he would record their face perfectly. The following day, if their hair had changed slightly or the lighting in the room was different, his brain would think it was a new person he'd never met before.

23

THE MIND READERS

If you ask me, this whole topic should be classified. The science of mind-reading could be pretty dangerous if it fell into the wrong hands. So be careful with this stuff!
Mind reading began in the 1920s, when the inventor William Marston built a machine called a polygraph. He claimed it could identify if people were telling the truth or not. Marston believed his lie detector machine could help the police solve crimes.

LIE DETECTORS

Lie detectors measure heart rate, breathing and sweat levels, but those things might be going haywire because the person is nervous, not because they're lying. Wouldn't you start sweating uncontrollably if someone tied you up to a machine and asked you to reveal your deepest darkest secrets?

WHAT'S ON YOUR MIND?

Although the lie detector machine didn't quite achieve its mind-reading mission, there might be other ways to 'read' minds. Every neuron in your brain is constantly sending electrical signals to other neurons around it. But different groups of neurons get more active when you're having different thoughts. Some neuron clusters get excited when you're trying to do maths, some get excited when you're trying to remember directions. If we can identify which neuron cluster goes with which type of thought, we might be able to guess what the brain is thinking.

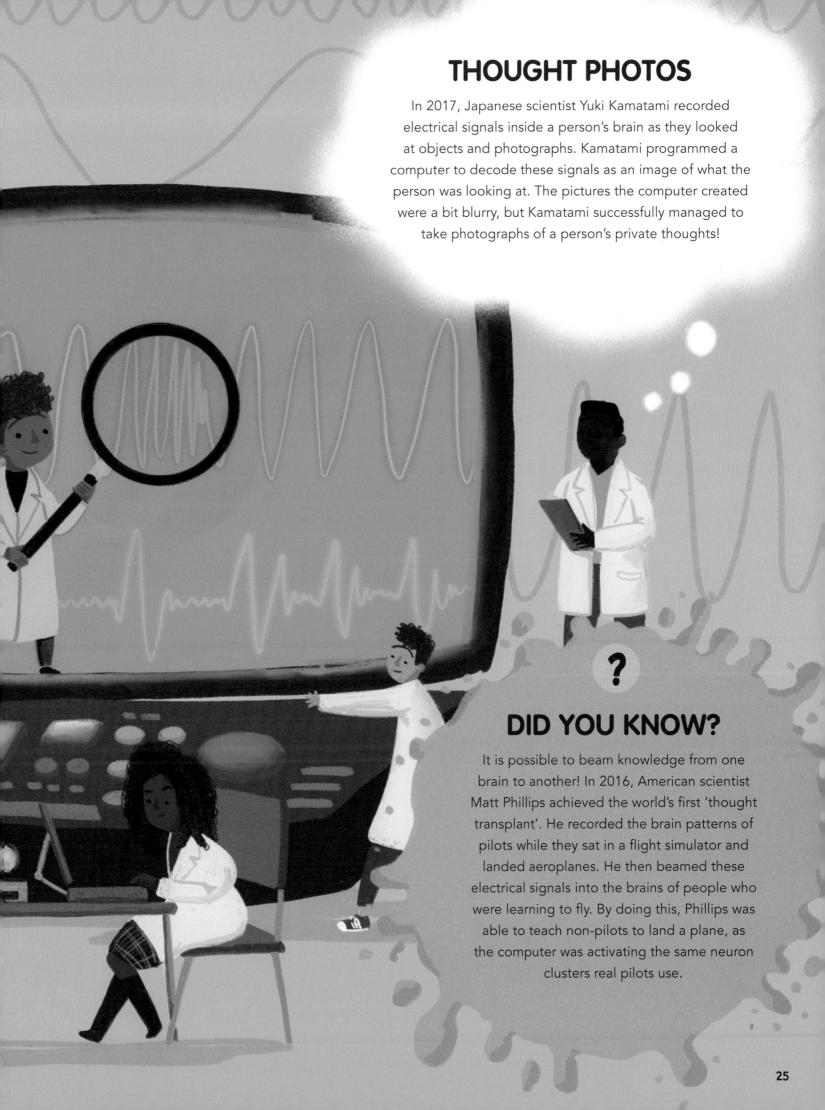

THOUGHT PHOTOS

In 2017, Japanese scientist Yuki Kamatami recorded electrical signals inside a person's brain as they looked at objects and photographs. Kamatami programmed a computer to decode these signals as an image of what the person was looking at. The pictures the computer created were a bit blurry, but Kamatami successfully managed to take photographs of a person's private thoughts!

?

DID YOU KNOW?

It is possible to beam knowledge from one brain to another! In 2016, American scientist Matt Phillips achieved the world's first 'thought transplant'. He recorded the brain patterns of pilots while they sat in a flight simulator and landed aeroplanes. He then beamed these electrical signals into the brains of people who were learning to fly. By doing this, Phillips was able to teach non-pilots to land a plane, as the computer was activating the same neuron clusters real pilots use.

THE TASTEFUL CHAPTER

Haha! Get it? Tasteful? I'm totally hilarious. Figuring out what food you're eating is really important because your brain uses it to detect whether you're eating something dangerous, or if you're getting enough of a particular chemical in your diet.

IT STARTS WITH THE MOUTH

Inside your mouth there are somewhere between 5,000 and 10,000 cells called taste receptors that get triggered by different chemicals. They're mostly on your tongue, but there are a few at the back of your throat and on the roof of your mouth too.

When you put a food containing one of these chemicals into your mouth, these receptors send electrical signals to the gustatory cortex in your frontal lobe where you decide what you're tasting. Unlike your olfactory cortex, which can detect over a trillion scents, your gustatory cortex can only detect five chemicals, meaning there are really only five tastes – sour, bitter, sweet, salty and umami (savoury).

SWEET

SOUR

UMAMI

You might have heard that different parts of the tongue are in charge of different tastes, but this isn't true at all. Your whole tongue is covered in the five types of taste receptor. The reason your brain thinks there are more than five different tastes is because when you put food in your mouth your nose is also detecting the chemicals, so you're smelling it at the same time. Both the gustatory and olfactory cortexes mash the information together to create the 'flavours' of food.

CAN YOU BE TASTELESS?

Some pop stars are. Haha! Joke! But seriously, it's a good question. It's extremely rare for your gustatory complex to not work, but it does occasionally happen. A small number of people, including Olympic gold medallist James Cracknell, have a condition called ageusia (ah-gyoo-zee-uh) where they can't taste food at all.

Many people also experienced the loss of their sense of taste when infected with the COVID-19 virus.

FEELING HOT

Sometimes when you're working on a case it's good to grab a snack. Fancy something with a bit of a kick? How about one of the world's spiciest chilli peppers? 'Pepper X', created by a professional chilli grower named Ed Currie back in 2017, is so powerful that if you ate a whole one it could make you seriously unwell. No? Not for you?

We can all recognise when something is spicy, but spiciness isn't actually a taste at all. In your cheeks are a bunch of sensors called TRPV1s that are in charge of detecting temperature. Unfortunately, these sensors are similar in shape to a chemical called capsaicin (caps-eye-sin), which is found in food such as chilli peppers. So when you eat these foods, your TRPV1s get activated and tell your brain that your mouth is hot, even though your tongue isn't detecting any temperature change at all. This 'hot-but-not-really' signal is what your brain calls 'spicy'.

GETTING EMOTIONAL

A big difference between the brain and a computer is that brains don't just store memories and solve puzzles – they experience emotions. We can 'feel' certain ways and that can be extremely powerful. I've got a feeling we can figure this out!

WHY DO YOU FEEL?

Nobody knows where emotions come from. What we do know is that when someone is having particular emotions, we find higher levels of certain chemicals called neurotransmitters in their brain. We don't know if the brain releases these chemicals and that's what causes the emotion, or if emotions happen and that causes the chemicals to increase. We just know there's a strong link between the two.

Let your feelings out!

These are the most common neurotransmitter chemicals.

ACETYLCHOLINE
Learning and remembering.

SEROTONIN
Relaxation, contentment and feeling calm.

GLUTAMATE
Focus and learning.

DOPAMINE
Excitement, motivation and pleasure.

ADRENALINE
Excitement, fear and anger.

NERVOUS REACTION

Neurotransmitters can have other strange effects on your body. Adrenaline can make you excited and increase your heart rate, but also make you lose bowel control. This is because if you're being chased by a tiger you need the energy to run away but also the back-up plan of going to the toilet all over yourself so the tiger won't eat you!

?

DID YOU KNOW?

The neurotransmitter serotonin is also found in your gut and when you eat certain foods, your gut bacteria might be producing more of it to tell your brain to eat more. Did you really want to eat that doughnut or did the bacteria in your intestines tell you to?

The Woman With No Fear

It's time to meet a woman code-named SM-046. Her real name is kept as a closely guarded secret by her doctors. All that's known officially about her is that she's a mother of three who lives in Kentucky, USA, and she has a very unusual brain.

In her childhood, she had a disease that damaged the part of the brain in charge of making you feel frightened. Scientists tested her lack of fear by showing her horror movies and seeing if she could handle snakes and spiders, but they didn't get a reaction!

WHAT ARE YOU SCARED OF?

Fear is an important emotion because it stops us from doing dangerous things. It's only a problem when you start being frightened of things that aren't dangerous. This is called a phobia and here are some examples.

ARACHIBUTYRIPHOBIA
Fear of peanut butter.

ARACHNOPHOBIA
Fear of spiders.

CYNOPHOBIA
Fear of dogs.

CHRONOMETROPHOBIA
Fear of clocks.

OPHIDIOPHOBIA
Fear of snakes.

NYCTOPHOBIA
Fear of the dark.

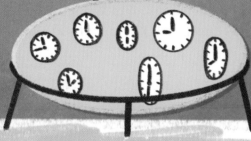

⌐HAVE YOU GOT THE TOUCH?⌐

Although the brain is probably the most important organ in your body, the largest organ is actually your skin! The skin is in charge of protecting you from infections, holding your insides together and of course, helping you detect how things feel. Your skin is a detective too!

HOW DOES YOUR BRAIN GET TOUCHY?

Just like the other four senses, touch has its own region of the brain called the sensory cortex. It gets its information from nerves located all over your skin, as well as organs inside your body. Most of your nerve sensors are in charge of sensing damage, which your brain interprets as pain, or mild irritation, which your brain interprets as itching. The reason scratching stops something from itching is because the pain of scratching your skin overloads the irritation signals and re-sets them back to zero (as well as removing whatever tiny thing was causing the itch in the first place – usually dried sweat or dust).

Scritch Scratch

OUT OF TOUCH

Lacking a sense of touch is a condition called 'anaphia', which is usually caused by serious damage to your spine that stops the signals getting from your body to your brain. This means you wouldn't know when you're hungry because you can't feel anything going on in your stomach, and you wouldn't be able to feel when your feet are touching the ground. Imagine trying to go upstairs with both your feet feeling numb all the time! Even a simple thing like going to the shops could be hard because you would have to constantly look at your feet to know when you'd taken a step.

WEIRD FEELINGS

The sensory cortex can do some pretty weird things too. When people have a limb removed they no longer have nerves where the limb used to be, but the brain's sensory cortex still has the neurons for that part of the body. About 80 per cent of amputees occasionally get pains or itches in what feels like their missing limb because the part of the brain in charge of it is still active! This is a condition called 'phantom limb syndrome'.

Even weirder is something called 'allochiria' where your touch senses send their electrical signals to the wrong side of the brain, meaning you can be touched on the left of your body but feel it happening on the right side!

?

DID YOU KNOW?

The least sensitive part of the body is your torso, while the most concentrated area is your fingertips, with each one containing about 3,000 nerve-sensors!

THE SIXTH. SEVENTH AND EIGHTH SENSES

We're acting as detectives of the brain, but the brain itself is like a detective – constantly trying to figure out what's going on around you. The five obvious senses – sight, hearing, smell, taste and feeling – are the ones you've heard about, but there are many more that you might not know!

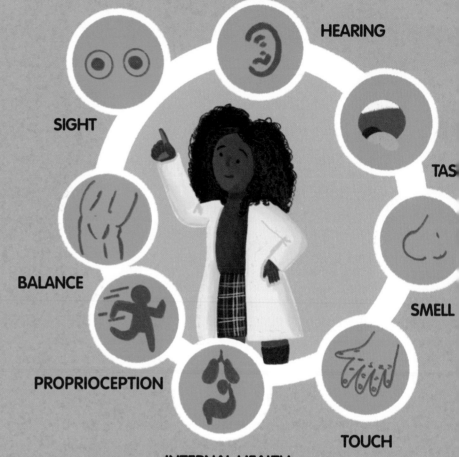

HEARING

SIGHT

TAS

BALANCE

SMELL

PROPRIOCEPTION

TOUCH

INTERNAL HEALTH

WHERE ARE YOU?

I want you to try a simple little experiment. Close your eyes and try waving your arms about all over the place. I'll bet you can still tell exactly where your arms are even though you're not looking at them and they're not touching anything. That's because your brain is able to detect the location of your own body parts – this is called proprioception (proe-pree-oh-sep-shun). Proprioception is controlled by a clump of neurons just inside your ear.

It's also in charge of figuring out how fast you're moving. But it can get mixed up with the other senses really easily. If you're sitting in a car, your proprioception can tell that you're sitting still because the car around you feels still, but your eyes are seeing everything moving by really fast. Your brain gets a confusing signal that you're both moving and not moving which is what causes people to feel travel sick.

GIDDY WITH EXCITEMENT

Similar to proprioception is your sense of balance. This is mostly controlled by neurons in the brainstem, although the electrical information comes from parts of the ear called the utricle and the saccule, which have a tiny compartments full of liquid and crystals with a bunch of hairs sticking into them. When your body tilts one way or the other, these hairs get brushed by the crystals in a certain direction, telling them which way your head is pointing.

When you spin around really fast, the liquid inside your ear sloshes with you and sends a signal to the brain that you're moving. When you stop, your eyes can see everything is still but the liquid in your ear is still spinning like a whirlpool, so your brain gets opposite signals again, creating the feeling of dizziness.

SOMEONE PASS ME A TOWEL

You also have the ability to detect temperature, although that sense can get a little overactive when the temperature changes and it thinks things are getting colder or hotter than they are. That's why you feel really cold stepping out of the shower even if the room is warm. Your temperature sense starts panicking and thinks, 'uh oh, the temperature's dropping, we're going to freeze to death!'

You've also got the ability to sense the passing of time, and even some senses you aren't aware of, like the ability to tell if you have too much of a particular chemical in your blood. We don't really know how many senses we have in total and will probably discover more in the future!

Brrrr

DID YOU KNOW?

Some animals (such as pigeons) can detect magnetic fields and they use this sense to navigate their way around the sky.

THE PEOPLE WHO SEE SOUND AS COLOUR

Regardless of how many senses you've got, different parts of your brain are in charge of understanding each one. But what's really cool is that sometimes these parts can get mixed together, leading to some pretty weird experiences. Let's investigate!

THE COLOUR OF MUSIC

Here's an interesting investigation to try – ask people what colour a high-pitched note is compared to a low-pitched note. Most people say high notes remind them of lighter colours while lower notes make them think of dark colours. Sound and sight are separate senses, but most people blur them together in their brain because the cortexes overlap slightly.

You can even make something taste different depending on how you serve it. Hot chocolate served in an orange or cream-coloured cup makes a lot of people enjoy the taste more than if you serve it in a red or white mug. Most people prefer to eat food that is laid out nicely too. There's no reason a waiter shouldn't just slop everything together into a bucket – it would taste the same – but our brains muddle up taste and sight so people think nicely presented food is better.

GOOD-LOOKING FOOD

Some people can detect senses simultaneously. The musician Billie Eilish says that when she's writing a song she can see the notes as well as hear them. She, like 15 per cent of people, has a brain that blurs senses – a condition called synaesthesia (sin-ess-thee-zee-uh).

Someone with synesthesia might find that when they hear particular noises or words they taste something at the same time. Or feel a sensation on their skin when they see certain objects or colours. The reason this happens is because the neurons in their cortexes are mixed up, meaning that when one gets activated, the other does too.

YOU MIGHT HAVE IT!

A lot of people have mild forms of synesthesia without realising. If I use the phrase, 'this vinegar tastes sharp' you probably know what it means even though your senses of touch and taste are not connected. No food actually cuts your mouth, but it still sort of makes sense.

You can even trick people's emotions with senses. If someone is holding a cold object when they meet you they often decide you're not very nice, while people holding warm objects tend to think the person they're talking to is friendly. So there's a tip. If you've got to give someone bad news, make them a cup of hot chocolate, and serve it in an orange mug!

THE BRAIN THAT PLAYED TRICKS

It's actually scary how easy it is to trick the brain. You don't even have to do much for your senses to start imagining things that aren't there, or to get muddled up about what's going on.

THAT'S DEDICATION

In 2016, a man named Alejandro Fragoso watched television for 94 hours straight. This might sound fun, but Alejandro did not enjoy it very much because his brain got so tired that it started making him hallucinate – hearing and seeing things in the room that weren't really there.

STREAMING INFORMATION

There's a part of your brain called the ventral stream that is constantly trying to decide what things are, which is why our brain is always looking to find patterns and shapes in things like clouds.

Sometimes it gets extreme. Prisoners who have been locked in dark rooms for several days start imagining things in the room with them, even entire television shows on the wall. Obviously, the guards haven't installed a flat-screen in their room – it's their brains inventing stuff because their rooms aren't providing anything interesting.

KANIZSA TRIANGLE

Take a look at this drawing. Your brain thinks there's a triangle in the centre, but there isn't. There are circles with chunks missing and unconnected lines around them. Your brain decides there's a triangle because the ventral stream is constantly trying to find information.

Pluto licked me!

🔍 **CASE STUDY**

Making up Memories at Disneyland

If you want to know something that will keep you awake at night there's the freaky fact that your brain can create fake memories – and you can't tell them apart from the real ones! In one experiment, people were asked to describe a holiday they'd taken to Disneyland. Soon after, they read a made-up news story about a man in a Pluto suit licking people's ears. A few weeks later, when asked to retell their holiday story, almost a third of the people claimed they had been licked by the man in the Pluto costume! Just reading about something had persuaded their brains to make up a fake memory.

HAVE YOU BEEN TRICKED?

If you think all your memories are real you might be right, but here's a few things to consider: the Kit Kat logo doesn't have a hyphen, the Monopoly man doesn't have a monocle, Pikachu's tail does not have a black tip, C-3PO has a silver leg and the evil queen in Snow White never says, 'Mirror, Mirror on the wall'. If you were shocked by any of those then you had a fake memory!

Can you see a vase or two heads on these pages? Is your brain playing tricks?

DECISIONS. DECISIONS ...

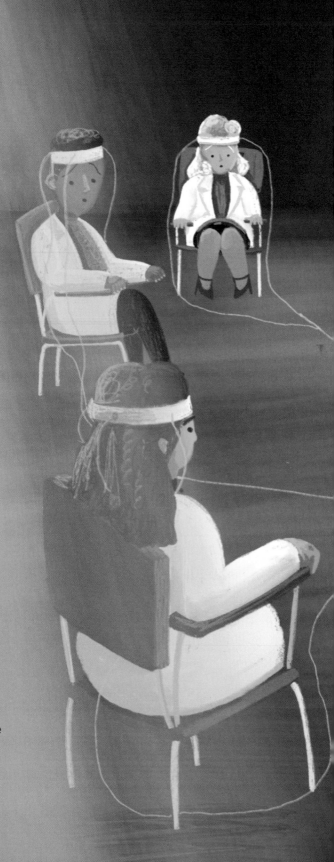

Every single day you make about 35,000 decisions. Often you do it without even realising. You decide what to wear, what to do, what to say and you make these choices incredibly quickly. How does your brain pick just one thing to do or say from the thousands of options available? The short answer is, we don't know. But there have been a few experiments that reveal something a bit scary. We might not be as in control of our choices as we think!

JOSÉ DELGADO

Time to meet one of the bravest brain detectives ever. José Delgado was a neuroscientist who went to incredible lengths to prove his discoveries to the public. In 1963, Delgado climbed into the ring with an angry bull and encouraged it to charge at him. As the crowd watched nervously, Delgado stood there without moving until the bull was almost upon him. But then, suddenly, as if by magic, the bull decided to stop and turn around. What on Earth happened?

Delgado had discovered that thoughts are electrical and that changing how the electricity flows through the brain can change the way you think. So, he placed a tiny electrical device into the bull's brain. Using a remote control, he was able to give the bull an electric shock at the very moment it was heading towards him, which made it change its mind.

Before using his device, which he called a stimociever (stim-oh-seevur) on the bull, Delgado tested it on humans. He asked volunteers to let him put the machine in their brain in the part in charge of movement. When he told them to sit still, they were unable to do it while he was triggering his device. Delgado was able to control people's decisions for them! Creepy!

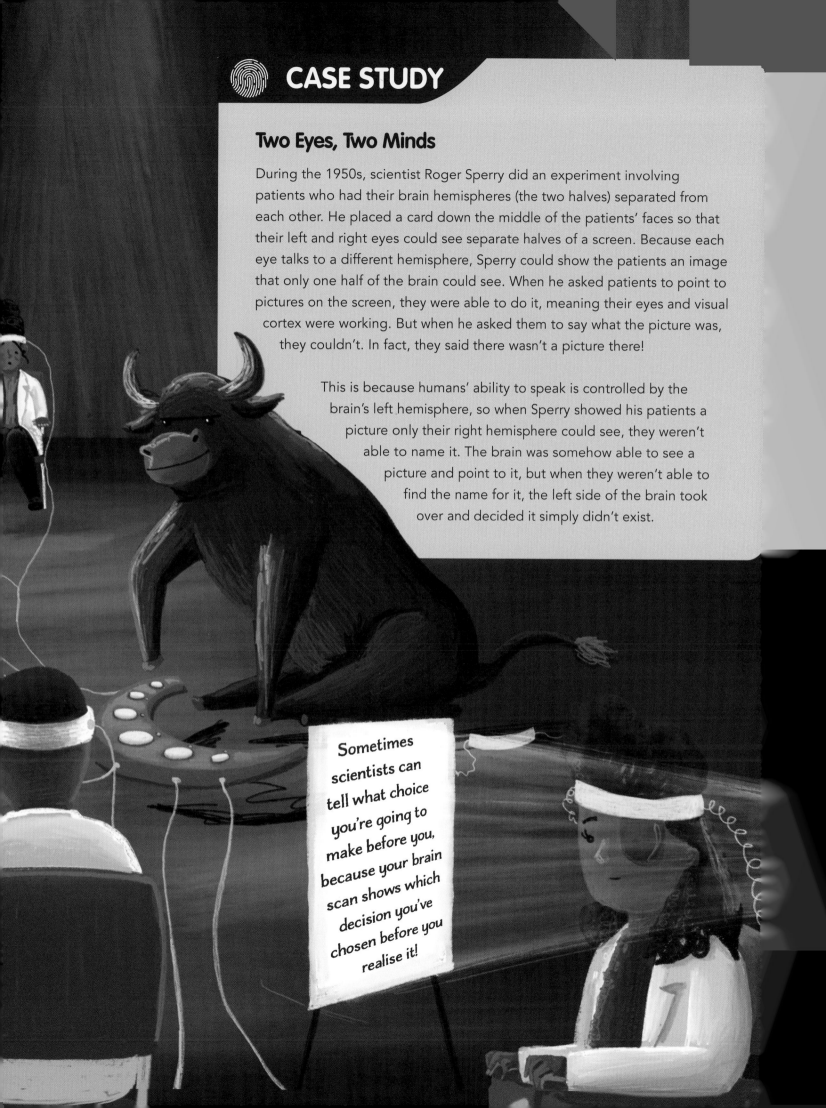

CASE STUDY

Two Eyes, Two Minds

During the 1950s, scientist Roger Sperry did an experiment involving patients who had their brain hemispheres (the two halves) separated from each other. He placed a card down the middle of the patients' faces so that their left and right eyes could see separate halves of a screen. Because each eye talks to a different hemisphere, Sperry could show the patients an image that only one half of the brain could see. When he asked patients to point to pictures on the screen, they were able to do it, meaning their eyes and visual cortex were working. But when he asked them to say what the picture was, they couldn't. In fact, they said there wasn't a picture there!

This is because humans' ability to speak is controlled by the brain's left hemisphere, so when Sperry showed his patients a picture only their right hemisphere could see, they weren't able to name it. The brain was somehow able to see a picture and point to it, but when they weren't able to find the name for it, the left side of the brain took over and decided it simply didn't exist.

Sometimes scientists can tell what choice you're going to make before you, because your brain scan shows which decision you've chosen before you realise it!

THE BRAIN IN THE JAR

When you meet someone who's really clever (such as super-sleuths like me) you might describe them as being 'brainy'. That's because intelligence is all to do with how well your brain does things. But where does intelligence come from?

THE GENIUS

I bet you've heard of the famous scientist Albert Einstein; he is often called the cleverest person of the twentieth century. Well, when Einstein died in 1955, Dr Thomas Harvey was desperate to examine his brain. So, he secretly removed the brain from Einstein's dead body, injected it with a chemical to preserve it, chopped it into 240 pieces, put it in two large jars of alcohol and stuck it in a box in his office. It was discovered 23 years later. (I wonder what Einstein would have thought about that . . . Probably not much . . . his mind was all over the place by that point.) So, is there anything weird about the brain of one of the cleverest people of all time? The answer is maybe.

CORPUS CALLOSUM
He had a thicker corpus callosum than normal (the bit that connects the two halves of the brain).

LATERAL SULCUS
Einstein was missing a piece of his brain called the lateral sulcus, which separates the frontal and parietal lobes from the temporal ones.

GLIAL CELLS
He had an unusually large number of glial cells (the care taker cells that keep the neurons clean).

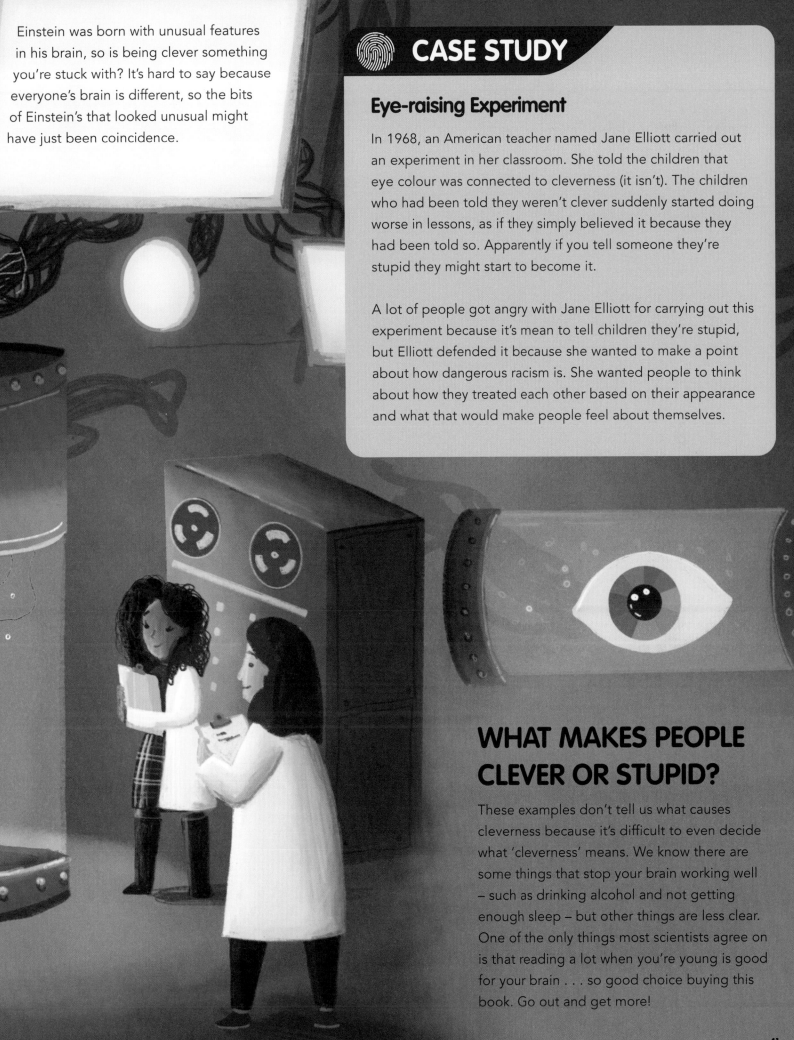

Einstein was born with unusual features in his brain, so is being clever something you're stuck with? It's hard to say because everyone's brain is different, so the bits of Einstein's that looked unusual might have just been coincidence.

CASE STUDY

Eye-raising Experiment

In 1968, an American teacher named Jane Elliott carried out an experiment in her classroom. She told the children that eye colour was connected to cleverness (it isn't). The children who had been told they weren't clever suddenly started doing worse in lessons, as if they simply believed it because they had been told so. Apparently if you tell someone they're stupid they might start to become it.

A lot of people got angry with Jane Elliott for carrying out this experiment because it's mean to tell children they're stupid, but Elliott defended it because she wanted to make a point about how dangerous racism is. She wanted people to think about how they treated each other based on their appearance and what that would make people feel about themselves.

WHAT MAKES PEOPLE CLEVER OR STUPID?

These examples don't tell us what causes cleverness because it's difficult to even decide what 'cleverness' means. We know there are some things that stop your brain working well – such as drinking alcohol and not getting enough sleep – but other things are less clear. One of the only things most scientists agree on is that reading a lot when you're young is good for your brain . . . so good choice buying this book. Go out and get more!

WHEN THE BRAIN TALKS

Right now you're reading this book by looking at shapes on the page (we ca[ll] them letters). Then, somehow, your brain is turning these shapes into idea[s] and thoughts! Let's investigate . . .

LEARNING A LANGUAGE

When babies are a few months old they start making babbling noises because they copy the sounds from adults around them. Babies of deaf or mute parents do something similar except they 'babble' with their hands, mimicking the sign-language symbols their parents use. Whether it's a spoken language or a hand-gesture one, babies start to learn you can communicate with symbols and after a few years they figure out which symbol matches which thought they have in their head.

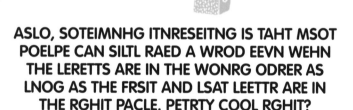

ASLO, SOTEIMNHG ITNRESEITNG IS TAHT MSOT POELPE CAN SILTL RAED A WROD EEVN WEHN THE LERETTS ARE IN THE WONRG ODRER AS LNOG AS THE FRSIT AND LSAT LEETTR ARE IN THE RGHIT PACLE. PETRTY COOL RGHIT?

DID YOU KNOW?

There are roughly 6,500 languages in the world and around 70 per cent of people speak at least two. The five most common are English, Mandarin Chinese, Hindi, Spanish and Arabic. The younger you start to learn a language, the easier you find it.

HOW DOES YOUR BRAIN SPEAK?

There are two main parts of the brain in charge of language: Wernicke's (Vur-nik-eez) area and Broca's (Broke-uz) area.

Wernicke's area is all to do with understanding the meanings of words. People who damage their Wernicke's area can put long sentences together but they don't mean anything, a bit like this: 'There isn't a negative slice of Philips who love the bouncy forks.'

Broca's area is more to do with understanding patterns in language, e.g. when to use 'are' and when to use 'is'. People who damage their Broca's area still understand the meanings of words, but they can't make full sentences and end up talking like a caveman: 'food . . . want . . . lots . . . now'.

Deaf and mute people use Broca's and Wernicke's areas in the same way as people who can hear and speak, which means language isn't really to do with sounds, it's to do with meanings and understanding them. There's even one language spoken in the valleys of La Gomera island called Silbo that is made up of whistled notes rather than spoken words!

Brain talks fast!

Hola!

CASE STUDY

The Boy Who Learned Spanish in a Coma

In 2016, a young man named Rueben Nsemoh was playing football when he got kicked in the head during a tackle and ended up in a coma. When he woke up though, Rueben was suddenly able to speak Spanish perfectly, even though he couldn't before. He had struggled with the language in school, but somehow the accident did something to his brain that helped him master it. In fact, the change was so dramatic that he even forgot how to speak English and it took him months to re-learn his original language! I'm actually quite jealous of him ... not because of the head injury, but I've been trying to learn Spanish for years and all I can do is count to five!

MIND OVER MATTER

Sometimes the power of the brain over the body is scary. Your brain can actually change your health and make you sick!

TALKED TO DEATH

One particularly scary story is about a man named Sam Shoeman who was treated for cancer in 1992. When his doctor told him he only had months left to live, Shoeman accepted the news and had one last Christmas with his family before returning to hospital on New Year's Day where he died 24 hours later. However, when his dead body was examined, it was discovered that the scan had been wrong. He did not have terminal cancer and had died, it would seem, because he had been told he was going to. See, it really is possible to talk someone to death!

WHAT'S GOING ON?

Nobody knows how this works but it's called the nocebo (no-see-bo) effect. For some people, their brain is so powerful it can actually make them sick just by thinking about it. It can work the other way round too, you can tell someone they've been given medicine and they start to get better because their mind makes it happen, this is called the placebo (pluh-see-bo) effect.

The Missing Poison

In 2007, Derek Adams went to hospital, panicking because he had taken too many pills for his medical condition. His blood pressure was dropping rapidly – he was showing symptoms of an overdose. However, when the doctors started looking for dangerous chemicals in his blood, they couldn't find anything. It was as if he had been poisoned, but the poison wasn't there. It turned out his doctor had been giving him sugar pills instead of medicine. There was no reason for him to be overdosing because he hadn't taken anything dangerous to overdose on!

As soon as Adams was told he hadn't been taking real medicine, his blood pressure went back to normal and he started to feel better, realising all he'd done was swallow 29 sweets. Hmmmm, perhaps eating too many sweets can make someone sick!

USING THIS EFFECT FOR GOOD

The brain's control over the body doesn't have to just lead to spooky and scary stories. In fact, in 2017, a doctor named Rupert Reichart was even able to perform surgery on a patient without anaesthetic to block their pain. Instead, Reichart was able to convince the patient they weren't getting any pain signals from their nerves . . . and it worked!

This is why doctors encourage people to have a cheerful outlook when they're sick. Telling yourself you feel better can be a treatment itself. It doesn't work for every illness – you can't fix a broken bone by telling yourself it's fine – and it works better in some people than others, but a lot of problems can be treated or caused just by thinking about them.

WHAT MAKES YOU 'YOU'?

Everyone has a slightly different personality. But why is that? What makes some people cheerful and others grumpy? Why are some people confident and some people shy? What makes you 'you'? This one gets complicated . . .

CASE STUDY

Two Jims

In 1979, two identical twin brothers, Jim Lewis and Jim Springer, who had been separated at birth, met up for the very first time. They had grown up in different parts of the USA and been raised by different families with different lives, yet they had some amazing similarities.

Both brothers enjoyed the same foods, went on holiday to the same beach every year, drove the same type of car, had the same type of job and both married a woman called Betty . . . before getting divorced and marrying another woman called Linda. Twins often have similar habits, hobbies and lifestyles because they have the same parents and inherit a lot of the same features, including features in the brain.

We do!

IS YOUR MIND FIXED AT BIRTH?

Well, that's not the whole story. The country you live in, the school you go to, the language you speak, the friends you make and the things that happen in your life also affect who you are. This is because every event in your life makes your brain change slightly to handle it. Part of who you are and how you think is the result of your surroundings and how you're raised.

 CASE STUDY

The Pirahã Children

Along the banks of the Maici River in Brazil there are a group of people called the Pirahã who have their own number system. They have two words hói (which means a few) and hoí (which means a lot). Children who grow up in Pirahã families have probably never come across the idea of maths.

However, Pirahã children are gifted hunters and are also able to create complicated and clever ways of finding food in the jungle – which you probably wouldn't be able to do, even if you are a whizz at maths. Intelligence takes different forms, and is measured differently depending on your experiences.

 CASE STUDY

The Boy Who Lived With Monkeys

In 1987, a five-year-old boy named Saturday Mthiyane was found living with monkeys in South Africa. Nobody knows where Saturday came from, but the monkeys had raised him for years and he grew up acting just like them. He would walk and jump like a monkey, communicate like a monkey and he ate food that monkeys eat. Who you are is partly down to who you spend your time with and how they behave!

BRAIN MAINTENANCE

Your brain and my brain are organs just like any other body part and we need to look after them. There are a few really important things you can do to make sure your mind is being taken care of, and the good news is that mostly they're pretty easy – it's the same stuff you do to keep the rest of your body healthy!

SLEEP

Get lots of sleep. Nobody likes being told it's their bedtime, but if you miss a lot of sleep it's not good for your brain. You might have heard that you need eight hours of sleep a night, but this is only rough guidance ... scientists disagree on how many hours different people should get. Just make sure you're resting as much as your body needs.

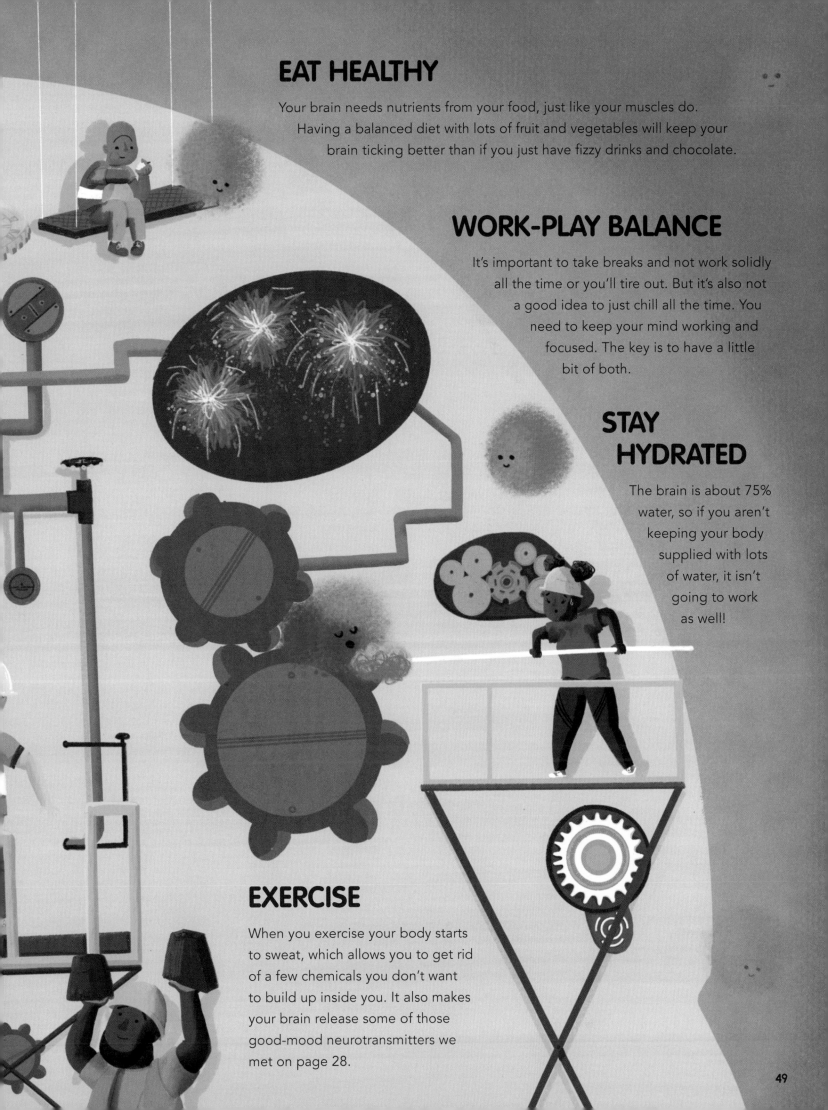

EAT HEALTHY

Your brain needs nutrients from your food, just like your muscles do. Having a balanced diet with lots of fruit and vegetables will keep your brain ticking better than if you just have fizzy drinks and chocolate.

WORK-PLAY BALANCE

It's important to take breaks and not work solidly all the time or you'll tire out. But it's also not a good idea to just chill all the time. You need to keep your mind working and focused. The key is to have a little bit of both.

STAY HYDRATED

The brain is about 75% water, so if you aren't keeping your body supplied with lots of water, it isn't going to work as well!

EXERCISE

When you exercise your body starts to sweat, which allows you to get rid of a few chemicals you don't want to build up inside you. It also makes your brain release some of those good-mood neurotransmitters we met on page 28.

49

BRAIN DETECTIVES TO THE RESCUE

The brain can also be affected by mental health difficulties. But thanks to the work of us brain detectives, doctors know enough about the brain to treat most common mental health difficulties.

WHY DOES IT HAPPEN?

All sorts of things can cause mental health difficulties. Some people's brains get sick because something bad or stressful has happened to them. Some people get sick because they're taking drugs that alter the way the brain is trying to work, like alcohol. But sometimes people just get sick without an obvious reason.

? DID YOU KNOW?

People are sometimes nervous to talk about mental health difficulties because they are worried others might label them 'crazy' or treat them differently. But mental health difficulties are very common, and almost everyone gets better eventually. So, if it happens to you, you're not alone. But if you start to feel like something is wrong, then it's very important to talk to an adult you trust.

IT'S GOOD TO TALK

Sitting down and having a chat with someone about how they feel can make a big difference. So, y'know, if a friend of yours doesn't seem like they're ok … ask them if they need to talk. They might be feeling a bit down or worried about something, and simply talking about it could make all the difference.

Sometimes though, the brain needs more help than a friend, parent or teacher can give. And that's where counsellors come in. Counsellors are trained to help you talk about how you feel, and they can give you advice and activities that will help you manage those feelings day-to-day.

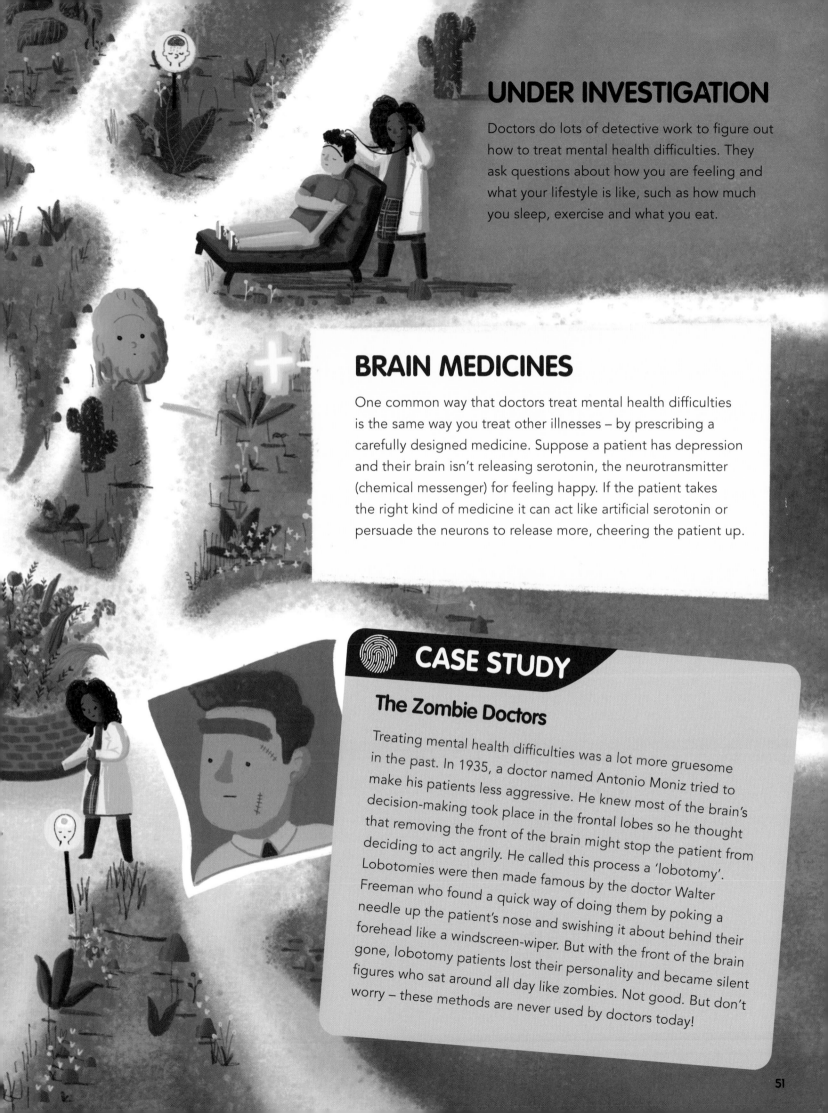

UNDER INVESTIGATION

Doctors do lots of detective work to figure out how to treat mental health difficulties. They ask questions about how you are feeling and what your lifestyle is like, such as how much you sleep, exercise and what you eat.

BRAIN MEDICINES

One common way that doctors treat mental health difficulties is the same way you treat other illnesses – by prescribing a carefully designed medicine. Suppose a patient has depression and their brain isn't releasing serotonin, the neurotransmitter (chemical messenger) for feeling happy. If the patient takes the right kind of medicine it can act like artificial serotonin or persuade the neurons to release more, cheering the patient up.

CASE STUDY

The Zombie Doctors

Treating mental health difficulties was a lot more gruesome in the past. In 1935, a doctor named Antonio Moniz tried to make his patients less aggressive. He knew most of the brain's decision-making took place in the frontal lobes so he thought that removing the front of the brain might stop the patient from deciding to act angrily. He called this process a 'lobotomy'. Lobotomies were then made famous by the doctor Walter Freeman who found a quick way of doing them by poking a needle up the patient's nose and swishing it about behind their forehead like a windscreen-wiper. But with the front of the brain gone, lobotomy patients lost their personality and became silent figures who sat around all day like zombies. Not good. But don't worry – these methods are never used by doctors today!

THE PLASTIC BRAIN

We've already investigated how different parts of the brain can have different jobs. What's really clever about the brain, though, is that it can change things around and re-shape itself when needed. Scientists call this amazing feature 'neuroplasticity'.

NEURONS CAN CHANGE

Do you remember the squiggly branches, called dendrites, that are on the ends of your neurons? We looked at them on page 7. Well, dendrites can grow in all sorts of directions, and form new links to other neurons all the time. This process is called 'dendritic branching', and it means your brain can keep coming up with new electrical patterns when it needs them.

The opposite thing can happen too through a process called 'synaptic pruning'. When you no longer need a certain skill or memory, dendrites begin to decay and eventually stop working altogether. This makes space for all the new things you're going to learn.

In fact, every single day your brain is slightly different to the day before because new dendrite patterns are being created all the time. You're a slightly new person every time you wake up!

IT'S GOOD TO BE YOUNG

Children's neural patterns can be moulded much more easily than adults', which is why children and young people learn new skills much more quickly. It also means it's easier to get a child to change their mind about something. Whereas, adults are more likely to be stuck in their ways!

CASE STUDY

The Girl With Half a Head

If someone's heart or lungs aren't working, you can sometimes give them a new one. But we don't have the technology to do that with a brain. Nobody has ever carried out a human brain transplant. Although, in 1970, Dr Robert White successfully transplanted a monkey's head from one body to another. No one has tried anything like this on humans yet, but there are some weird brain surgeries . . .

This brings me to the case of Jodie Miller, who suffered from a rare condition that made her brain swell against her skull. The doctors removed the swollen half of her brain – the right side. Remarkably, Jodie's left hemisphere started re-wiring itself to take on the job of both halves. Jodie went on to live a totally normal life and talking to her you'd have no idea one half of her head is empty! How amazing is that?

THE BRAINS IN THE TREES AND THE WAVES

There are 8.7 million different species of animal on Earth, and those are just the ones we know about. How animals' brains work is one of the biggest mysteries.

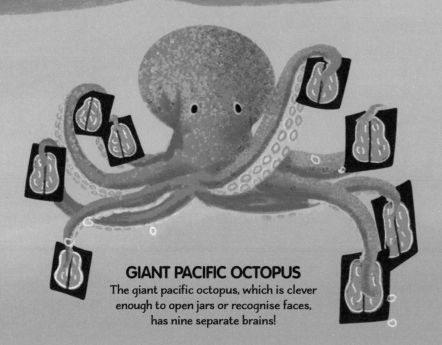

GIANT PACIFIC OCTOPUS
The giant pacific octopus, which is clever enough to open jars or recognise faces, has nine separate brains!

HUMBLE JELLYFISH
The humble jellyfish doesn't have a brain at all. Instead, it has neurons spread out all over its body.

MANTIS SHRIMP
The mantis shrimp can see four times as many colours as we can.

SHARK
Sharks have an extra sense that can pick up electricity.

DO ANIMALS THINK LIKE US?

It's impossible for us to imagine how other animals think because their brains are so different. And it's not like we can ask them because they don't speak any of our human languages. What we know for sure is that other animal's brains are built similarly to ours, with the same kinds of neurons and neurotransmitters. Unlike humans, however, most animals don't have a complicated neo-cortex outer layer – the part of the human brain that does all our advanced thinking and feeling. This means other animals might not have the same complicated types of thought we do. A cat might feel similar things to us, like desire for food or wanting to avoid pain, but you don't see many cats writing books or making scientific discoveries.

HONEY, I'M HOME

Honeybees have one of the most unusual types of animal-thinking. When honeybee scouts want to tell the other bees where to find honey, they perform funny 'waggle dances'. They shake their bums in a figure of eight. The length of the dance tells other bees how far to fly and the angle of their dance represents the nectar's location. Other bees can then calculate the location of the nectar from this information, which is pretty clever.

And to make it even more exciting, bees compete against each other. Sometimes, two rival bees will do their own dance at the same time and members of the hive then decide who to trust. That's right! Bees communicate using mathematical bum-dance battles! I've tried suggesting this to other scientists I know, so far no one seems very keen.

BUTTERFLIES
Butterflies smell through their feet.

Sniff

Let's dance!

Can I scan your brain, please?

UNDER THE SEA

Whales and dolphins do seem to have the same complicated wrinkled brain layers we do, but it's impossible to run a brain scan on them to see how they think . . . brain-scanning machines tend not to work so well underwater!

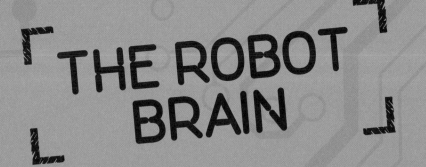

THE ROBOT BRAIN

People have been trying to make artificial brains for decades, but one of the reasons they've never come close is because a lot of what the brain does is a mystery! It's tricky to copy something when you don't know how it actually works in the first place.

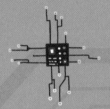

CAN WE SIMULATE THE HUMAN BRAIN?

In 2012, the Japanese company Fujitsu built a supercomputer called 'The K' that was so big it had to be built in a warehouse. The K could simulate roughly 1.73 billion neurons, but the human brain has around around 86 billion neurons. In other words: even a computer the size of a warehouse can only simulate 2% of a human brain.

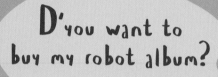

Deep Blue

HOW CLOSE HAVE WE GOT?

So far, there isn't a computer that can copy human thought, but they can copy some of its functions. The face-recognition in a smartphone, the voice-recognition in a smart-hub, even the characters in video games are examples of computers learning to do things we can.

? DID YOU KNOW?

In 1997, a computer called Deep Blue was designed to play chess – and it defeated the human world chess champion, Gary Kasporov, in three games out of six. In 2009, another computer called Emily Howell was designed to compose music. Not only has 'Emily' fooled music experts into believing it's a real person, but Emily also released an album.

WHY CAN'T WE JUST BUILD A ROBO-BRAIN?

One of the big differences between brains and computers is that computers do things one step at a time. Even something like a video game, which looks like it has lots of things going on simultaneously, is just doing one task after another in sequence. Your brain, on the other hand, can do lots of things at the same time. It's what's called a 'parallel processor'.

THE BRAIN'S BIGGEST MYTHS

By now you know that the brain is rather mysterious. This is frustrating for people who like knowing everything, which means many of the things said about the brain are completely made up! Let's investigate some of the brain's biggest myths.

SOME PEOPLE ARE LEFT-BRAINED AND SOME ARE RIGHT-BRAINED

NOPE!

While some skills are more often found on one side of the brain than the other (the language bits are usually on the left, for instance), nobody uses one side of the brain more than the other.

Zzzzz

WE ONLY USE 10% OF OUR BRAINS

NO WAY!

Every neuron in your brain is active all the time – it's just that certain areas speed up and slow down during certain activities.

CAFFEINE HELPS YOU STAY AWAKE

SORT OF

Caffeine is a chemical found in coffee, tea, chocolate, cola and other energy drinks. It doesn't actually give you energy, but it does block the chemical in your brain that tells you that you're getting tired (adenosine). So, you only feel 'awake' because your body is ignoring the 'you should feel tired' warning.

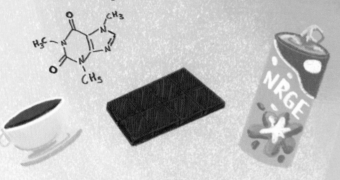

SUGAR MAKES YOU HYPER

BOGUS

This is an easy mistake to make. Sugar is a chemical with lots of energy inside it . . . but it's energy your body uses slowly to keep cells and muscles active, not to give you enthusiasm. When children are given sweets and get hyperactive afterwards, it's not the sugar doing it – it's the fact they've just been given sweets!

BRAIN CELLS DIE AS YOU GET OLDER

ERRR...

This one is mostly false, although there is a teeny-tiny bit of truth to it. You're born without your whole brain, and it doesn't finish growing until you're 25 years old. Once you get to that age though, your neurons don't just start dying. They can lose their connections to other neurons if they aren't used regularly, but if you keep your mind sharp and live a healthy lifestyle, your brain won't automatically start to lose neurons at all. In fact, you can actually grow more of them!

I may be old, but my brain is still quick!

THE UNSOLVED MYSTERIES

Brain detectives have learned about the brain already, but the good news is that most of it is still a complete mystery, which means there's so much we still have to discover! So, what are the next big mysteries about the brain we're nowhere near solving?

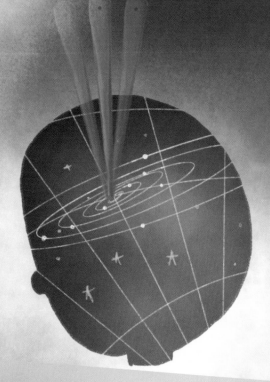

BIG MYSTERY 1
What is it Made Of?

We still don't know much about what the brain is even made of! Sure, we know it has neurons and glial cells . . . but we don't know how many varieties they come in. There are at least a dozen different types of neurons and we don't have a clue which ones interact with which.

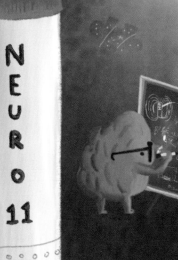

BIG MYSTERY 2
How Does it Solve Puzzles?

The brain doesn't just store a bunch of information like a file on a computer. It can learn new information, change what it knows, link things together and, most importantly, figure out things it doesn't already know. How does a big bag of salty water and fat somehow figure out how to build rockets, invent medicines and even understand the brain. Brain detectives are really brains studying brains . . . but how do their brains know how to do it?

IT'S GOOD TO HAVE A LITTLE MYSTERY

Everyone loves a good mystery, and the brain has mysteries within mysteries. When there are mysteries to be solved, scientists (who are the most dedicated detectives ever) will be there to try and crack them!

BIG MYSTERY 3
Where Does Consciousness Come From?

We can build computers that can store information and solve puzzles, but no computer is alive. No computer can 'feel' itself existing and be aware that it is a real thing. Yet somehow our brains can. Using nothing more than a few electrical signals, your brain can give you a sense of being a person in the past, present and future. How it does this is one of the biggest mysteries of all!

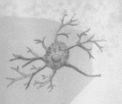

GLOSSARY

Acetylcholine – Hormone responsible for learning and remembering

Adrenaline - Hormone produced when you experience excitement, fear and anger

Allochiria – Condition where the touch senses send signals to the wrong side of the brain

Amusia – Condition whereby the brain can hear musical notes, but cannot detect tunes

Anaphia – Condition caused by damage to the spine that results in lack of touch

Arachnophobia – Fear of spiders

Arachibutyriphobia – Fear of peanut butter

Auditory – Things relating to the sense of hearing

Autopsy – Examination of a corpse to discover the cause of death

Axon – Thread-like part of a neuron

Brainstem – Bit of the brain that connects to the spine

Broca's area – One of two parts of the brain in charge of language

Caffeine – Chemical found in coffee, tea, chocolate, cola and energy drinks

Cerebellum – Part of your brain responsible for balance and movement

Cerebrum – Part of your brain where all your important thinking happens

Cochlea – Small bone found in the ear

Cone cells – Cells found in the eyes that are in charge of detecting colour

Consciousness – State of being aware of and responsive to one's surroundings

Corpus callosum – Bit that connects the two halves of the brain

Deep Blue – Computer designed to play chess

Dendrites – Branches of a neuron

Dopamine – Hormone responsible for excitement, motivation and pleasure

Ear drum – Part of the ear that vibrates in response to sound

Emily Howell - Computer designed to compose music

Glutamate – Hormone responsible for focus and learning

Gustatory – Things relating to the sense of taste

Hippocampus – Place in the brain where memories are stored

Hormones – Bodily chemical designed to do certain things, especially important for growing up

The K – Supercomputer built by Fujitsu that simulates 2% of a human brain

Lateral sulcus – Part of the brain that separates the frontal and parietal lobes

Lobe – Each of the parts of the brain

Lobotomy – Operation involving cutting into the prefrontal lobe of the brain

Mental health – Person's psychological and emotional well-being

Molecules - Tiny bits of chemicals

Nerves – Fibres that transmit electrical impulses to the brain and spine

Neuron – Cell that specializes in transmitting nerve impulses

Neuroscientist – Scientist who studies the brain

Nocebo effect – When people get ill because they believe themselves to be

Nucleus – Part of the cell that's in charge of building and telling the rest of the cell what to do

Olfactory – Things relating to the sense of smell

Ophidiophobia – Fear of snakes

Optic – Things relating to the sense of sight

Papyrus – Material used in ancient times for writing and painting on

Particles – Tiny portions of matter

Phantom limb syndrome – Condition where patients experience pain in a limb that does not exist

Phobia – Fear of something

Placebo effect – When someone starts to get better because they believe they have taken medicine

Polygraph – Lie-detector machine

Proprioception – Sense through which we detect the location of our body parts

Rapid eye movement (REM) sleep – Stage of sleep where dreams mostly occur

Sensory – Things relating to the sense of touch

Serotonin – Hormone responsible for relaxation, contentment and feeling calm

Stimociever – Device created by José Delgado that sends electrical signals to the brain

Synesthesia – Condition where the senses are blurred and often experienced together

Wernicke's area – One of the parts of the brain in charge of language

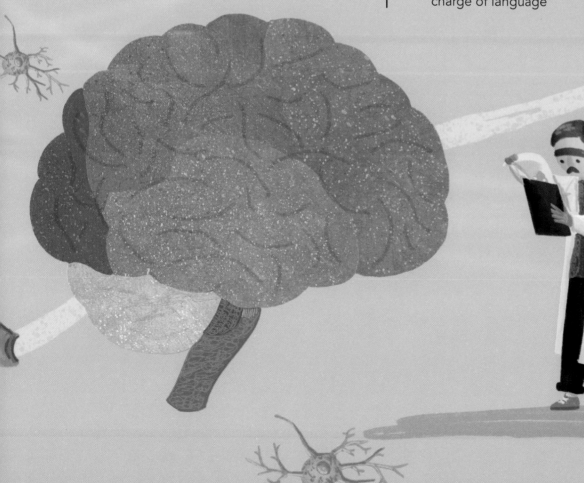